I0799522

THE VAJA

R024-221
Y-1371
وزارت دفاع
و پشتیبانی
نیروهای مسلح

THE VAJA

ODYSSEYS

TOMAS LORENZO

CREATIVE EDUCATION · CREATIVE PAPERBACKS

Published by Creative Education and Creative Paperbacks
P.O. Box 227, Mankato, Minnesota 56002
Creative Education and Creative Paperbacks
are imprints of The Creative Company
www.thecreativecompany.us

Design by Graham Morgan
Art direction by Tom Morgan
Edited by Jill Kalz

Images by Alamy Stock Photo/JAHANGIR RAZMI, 11; FBI/public domain, 72; Getty Images/AlexLinch, 60, Anadolu, 45, 56, Kaveh Kazemi, 14, NurPhoto, 38, zabelin, 28; Shutterstock/BalkansCat, 37, zieusin, 31; Unsplash/Alireza Esmaeeli, cover, 8, GR Stocks, 75, Philipp Katzenberger, 53, Towfiqu barbhuiya, 48; Wikimedia Commons/Bequest of George C. Stone, 4–5, Émile Bayard & Ármin Vámbéry, 6, farsi.khamenei.ir, 46, Gustave Doré, 70–71, Ichwan Palongengi, Svenskbygderna, 50, iichs.ir, 24, 64, Israel Defense Forces, 2, Ministry of Intelligence (Iran), 20, Mostafameraji, 34–35, Palotabarát, 54, public domain, 12, 19, 59, 63, 66, 69, Tasnim News Agency, 41, Xnet1234/Kan 11/Apple TV+/CC BY-SA 4.0, 27

Library of Congress Cataloging-in-Publication Data
Names: Lorenzo, Tomas, author.
Title: The VAJA / Tomas Lorenzo.
Description: Mankato, Minnesota : Creative Education and Creative Paperbacks, [2025] | Series: Odysseys in spycraft | Includes bibliographical references and index. | Audience: Ages 12–15 | Audience: Grades 7–9 | Summary: "Unlock the spy secrets of Iran's VAJA (also, MOIS), from the civilian espionage agency's history of intelligence gathering to its assassins and key missions. Includes a glossary, sidebars, index, and further resources"—Provided by publisher.
Identifiers: LCCN 2024020395 (print) | LCCN 2024020396 (ebook) | ISBN 9798889892946 (library binding) | ISBN 9781682776605 (paperback) | ISBN 9798889894056 (ebook)
Subjects: LCSH: Iran. Vizārat-i Ittilāʻāt va Amnīyat-i Kishvar—Juvenile literature. | Intelligence service—Iran—History—Juvenile literature.
Classification: LCC JQ1785.A55 I656 2025 (print) | LCC JQ1785.A55 (ebook) | DDC 327.1255009--dc23/eng/20240513
LC record available at https://lccn.loc.gov/2024020395
LC ebook record available at https://lccn.loc.gov/2024020396

Printed in the United States of America

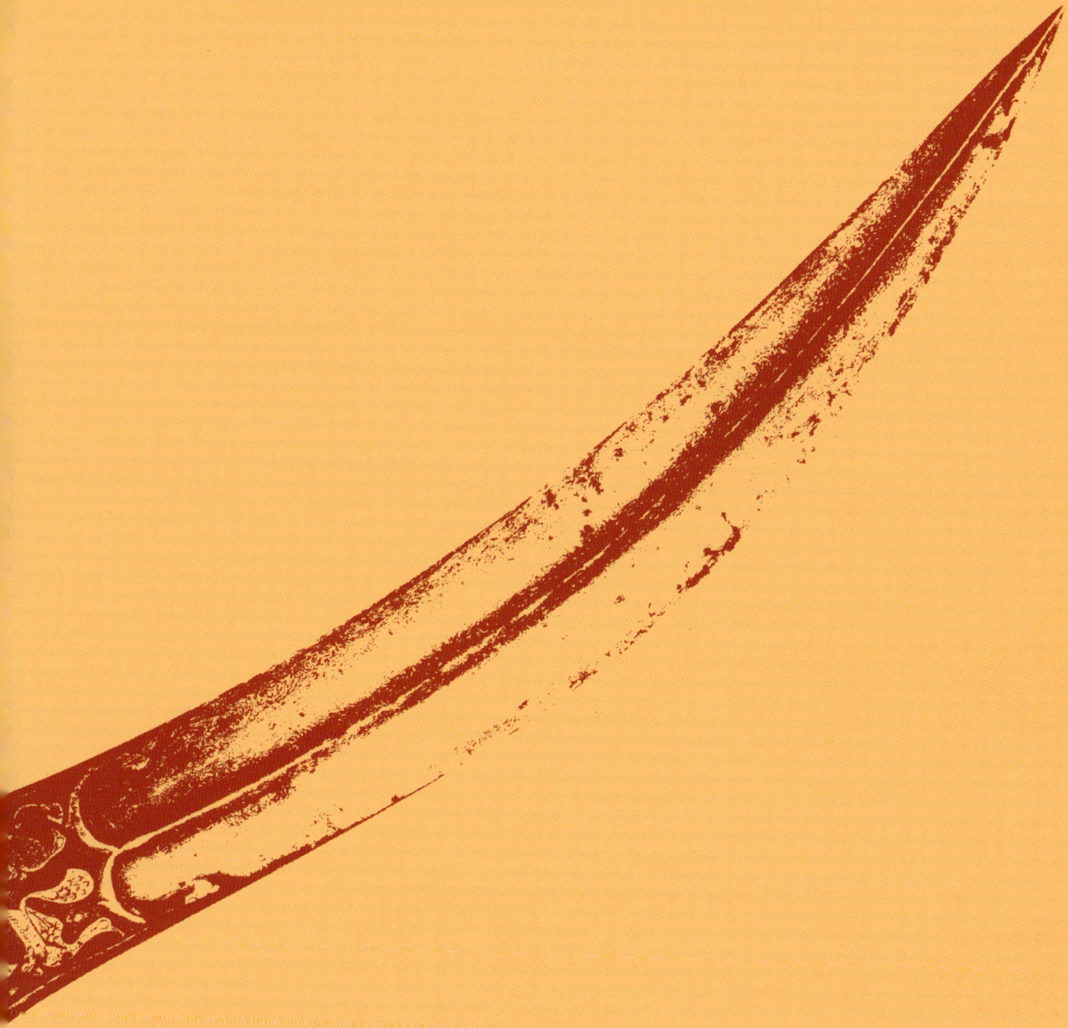

Spies in Central Asia, depicted by French illustrator Émile Bayard, 1863

CONTENTS

Introduction

Welcome to the secret world of Iran's Ministry of Intelligence and Security (MOIS), also known by its **Farsi** name and acronym, the Vezarat-e Ettela'at Jomhuri-ye Eslami-ye (VAJA). The primary mission of the VAJA is to keep the Islamic government in power by safeguarding the nation's interests at home and abroad.

OPPOSITE: Built in 1971, the Azadi Tower, or Tower of Freedom, is an architectural marvel in the center of Tehran, Iran.

As Iran's foremost civilian (non-military) **intelligence** agency, the VAJA is tasked with gathering and analyzing critical information necessary to the country's security, wherever that information may be found. Its legacy began in the aftermath of Iran's 1979 Islamic Revolution and the overthrow of Shah Mohammad Reza Pahlavi. As the newly established Islamic Republic sought to strengthen its standing and further the goals of the revolution, the need for a powerful, modern intelligence and security system became clear. Coupled with the backlash against the former government's secret police and intelligence agency, and the need for a professional, disciplined intelligence organization, the VAJA was born.

Enemies of the Islamic Revolution are executed in 1979.

OPPOSITE Ayatollah Ruhollah Khomeini founded the Islamic Republic of Iran and helped shape the VAJA.

The VAJA is a highly skilled, wide-reaching player in the world of domestic and international **espionage**. Drawing on a mix of traditional and modern methods, VAJA spies work in the shadows to safeguard the Islamic Republic from any existing or potential internal and external enemies. From gathering intelligence on political **dissidents** to countering foreign interference, the VAJA's reach extends across the globe.

۹۴۳۹۵۰

Founding and Origins

Iran's VAJA was established in 1983. It serves as the country's primary civilian intelligence agency. Its priority is domestic intelligence collection and the monitoring of dissident and opposition groups within Iran, such as the Mujahedin-e Khalq (MEK), an Iranian resistance group. But it also conducts foreign intelligence operations. It does this through units such as Department 15, which "liaisons with many types of resistance and terrorist movements throughout the world."

OPPOSITE: Members of MEK are dedicated to the overthrow of the Islamic Republic of Iran, making them VAJA targets.

VAJA agents are known as the "Unknown Soldiers of Imam Zaman." The name was given to them by former supreme leader Ayatollah Ruhollah Khomeini. Agents must be of the "Twelver" religious branch of Shia Islam, whose followers believe in the 12 divinely ordained leaders known as the Twelve Imams. Many VAJA agents are recruited from religious training schools, called seminaries, such as the Haqqani School in the holy city of Qom. Various Iranian leaders with "radical right" or more conservative political views have graduated from the Haqqani School. Thousands of former seminary students now work as intelligence officers in the shadows of foreign governments, militaries, and businesses around the world.

Even though the VAJA was established after the 1979 Islamic Revolution, discontent against the government of Shah Mohammad Reza Pahlavi was sown long beforehand. Years of strongly controlled rule combined with social and economic inequality created widespread resentment in Iran. The revolution, backed by Ayatollah Khomeini and other opposition groups, ended with the overthrow of the shah and the creation of an Islamic government.

Iran changed dramatically following the revolution. The country was in a state of internal unrest. The new government faced opposition both inside and outside its borders. The remnants of the former government's brutal and bloody security and intelligence agency, known as the SAVAK (a Farsi abbreviation for Sazman-e Ettela'at va Amniat-e Melli-e Iran), lingered. In such a dangerous environment, the Islamic Republic needed a powerful, modern intelligence agency to protect its interests. In the chaos and uncertainty of this time, the VAJA was created.

Several figures played important roles in the establishment of the VAJA, shaping its development and guiding its early years. One such figure was Ayatollah Khomeini,

Haqqani School co-founder Ali Qoddusi

Haqqani School

The Haqqani School, located in Qom, about 90 miles (145 kilometers) south of Tehran, is one of the most highly regarded Islamic seminaries in the world for Shia religious study and law. Established around the mid-20th century, the school attracts students and academics from the global Shia Muslim community. Courses range from basic studies of the Koran (the Muslim holy book) to high-level philosophy. Because the school's teachers are among the world's leading Shia scholars, students hold them in exceptionally high regard and feel privileged to be taught by them. Many graduates go on to become Iranian government officials, religious leaders, and intelligence officers charged with protecting Iran.

وزارت اطلاعات
جمهوری اسلامی ایران

VAJA Emblem

The VAJA's emblem includes several symbols related to the agency's national and religious beliefs. The eye with a globe as its pupil stands for watchfulness and represents the all-seeing eye of the intelligence agency tasked with protection of the Islamic Republic. The eye is embedded in a star with eight corners, colored in a deep green. Both the polygon and dark green are used as Islamic religious symbols. Finally, the traditional calligraphy on the emblem symbolizes the VAJA's Persian roots. In Farsi, it reads: "Islamic Republic of Iran, Ministry

the leader of the 1979 Islamic Revolution. His vision of an Islamic state guided the founding principles of the VAJA. It emphasized the need for an intelligence agency grounded in the principles of Islam and dedicated to protecting the revolution's goals.

Another key figure was Hojjat al-Islam Mohammad Montazeri. As the deputy to Ayatollah Khomeini, Montazeri played a crucial role in shaping Iran's post-revolutionary security systems. He helped formulate the structure and rules of the VAJA, ensuring that it remained loyal to the ideals of the revolution. Additionally, figures such as Ali Khamenei, who would later become Iran's supreme leader, and Akbar Hashemi Rafsanji, a well-known revolutionary figure, also played significant roles in the creation of the VAJA. Collectively, these men laid the groundwork for the intelligence agency that would be the eyes and ears of the young Islamic Republic.

The VAJA faced many challenges and obstacles at first. But with the energy and drive of its founders and their

“AN INTELLIGENCE AGENCY GROUNDED IN THE PRINCIPLES OF ISLAM AND DEDICATED TO PROTECTING THE REVOLUTION’S GOALS.”

unwavering commitment to the revolution’s objectives, the VAJA grew into a global secret intelligence operation. Its leaders and agents navigated political turmoil, international tensions, and regional conflict that would shape Iran’s history and the Middle East for years to come.

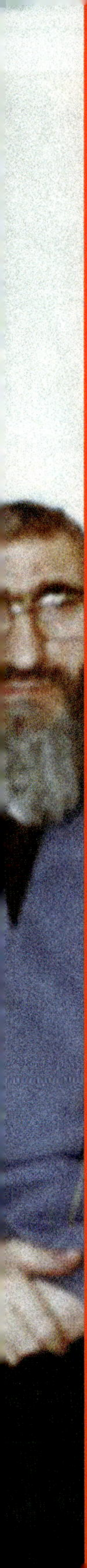

Reality vs. Fiction

The real-life experiences of VAJA's "unknown soldiers" seldom align with their portrayal in the media. The specific challenges and dangers faced by VAJA agents are not publicized. Their successes often go unmentioned, and their efforts are usually revealed only by their failures. In the world of espionage, where reality can blur with fiction, mystery and deception go hand in hand with the **tradecraft**. What people know about Iran's intelligence **operatives**, or what they *think* they know about them, is often only as much as the Islamic Republic wants them to know.

OPPOSITE: Religious scholars, called clerics, came to power following the 1979 Islamic Revolution and oversaw the creation of the VAJA.

OPPOSITE The TV series *Tehran* features Niv Sultan [*left*] as a spy for Israel's Mossad on a mission in the heart of Iran.

In Hollywood movies and television shows, Iran's intelligence operatives are often shown as shadowy figures. They're super villains or agents of an extremely controlling, brutal **regime** fixated on the destruction of Israel and the United States. In cloak-and-dagger television series, such as *Homeland* or *Tehran*, Iranian super spies are pitted against James Bond-like spies from Western intelligence agencies, including the CIA (United States), the Mossad (Israel), and the SIS (also called MI6; Great Britain). The ensuing shootouts, car chases, and suspense make for thrilling, action-packed entertainment. Frequently, fictional VAJA agents serve as short-fused masterminds or ruthless agents for the Iranian regime. They are pictured as tough, machinelike opponents who will do anything for Iran, whether it be assassinating foreign leaders or carrying out complex

Hollywood Muslims

Hollywood's portrayal of Muslims, particularly when it comes to Iranians, has been criticized for continuing to use clichés and preconceptions. It often depicts the community as primarily responsible for global terror and espionage. In the mainstream media, too, there is a tendency to treat all Muslims as radicals and extremists, thus downplaying the diversity of the Muslim identity. Although the Apple TV series *Tehran* shines a more optimistic light on Iranian culture and civilization, it still focuses on the anti-Western and anti-Israel ideologies of Iranian intelligence operatives, which only serves to affirm the aforementioned stereotypes. As a consequence, viewers are left with a limited view of Iranian Muslims and a less-than-accurate one. By focusing primarily on the political and religious aspects of Iran's intelligence and military operations, the series overlooks much of the cultural, social, and personal aspects of the lives of Iranian Muslims.

plots of mass destruction. These portrayals may hook audiences, but they often contradict reality.

There is a common thread running through such Hollywood depictions of the VAJA. It says that an agent's loyalty to the Islamic Republic and willingness to die for the cause of the Iranian Revolution is motivated more by conviction than self-interest. And while the VAJA does recruit most of its agents from conservative religious seminaries, not every agent is a "holy warrior" for Iran, as often shown in fictional stories. TV and movie

“THE VAJA OPERATES IN A HIGHLY POLITICIZED, DIVIDED ENVIRONMENT.”

depictions of the VAJA often feed into stereotypes and misperceptions. In reality, the VAJA is a multifaceted organization. It has a large pool of operatives of varying skill levels and expertise. Some operatives might have the cunning and resourcefulness that Hollywood suggests, but others are less skilled or motivated by personal ambition rather than any deep loyalty to the regime. Hollywood also glosses over the VAJA's limitations and vulnerabilities. It presents a picture of an all-powerful, flawless intelligence agency. In reality, however, the VAJA operates in a highly politicized, divided environment. It is troubled by internal rivalries, political problems,

Laser sights increase accuracy in low-light situations.

and external pressures, just like any other intelligence organization in the world.

Another common misstep in TV shows and movies originating in the West is the idea that the VAJA and its agents are simply extensions of the ruling class, not individuals. Though the VAJA serves the Iranian regime, its agents are not entirely without free will. They have their own beliefs, ambitions, and loyalties that sometimes do not exactly match those of the regime.

In the United States, television series and movies about Islamic spies tend to focus on black-and-white storylines. They feature exceptionally professional, quick-thinking Western or Israeli intelligence officers and shrewd, evil-minded, radical spies from Iran or other Middle Eastern countries. It's the old Hollywood standby: hero vs. villain. Every good classic story needs one or the other. When television and movie producers are from the West or Israel, they like to depict their own spies as the winners, of course.

When it comes to real-life intelligence work, though, the story isn't as black and white. *The New York Times* once analyzed leaked Iranian intelligence documents and noted that "the intelligence ministry operatives portrayed in the documents appear patient, professional,

Iran's holy Shrine of Hilal ibn Ali is a place for visitors to reflect and pray.

OPPOSITE The best spies are adept at blending in with crowds.

and pragmatic." The documents demonstrated Iran's outmaneuvering the United States in the competition for influence in Iraq at almost every turn. That wouldn't have been possible if Iranian spies were as unskilled as Hollywood often portrays them.

VAJA agents operate in a world where every mission could be their last. One of the biggest challenges they face is the constant threat of exposure. Unlike their fictional counterparts, who effortlessly move through glamorous mazes of deception and mystery,

VAJA operatives must train hard and be ever alert. In a country where dissent is met with harsh punishment, the stakes are incredibly high for VAJA agents, as well as their family members, both at home and abroad.

While much of how the VAJA operates is unknown and kept in the shadows, one thing is certain: VAJA intelligence officers, like all intelligence officers around the world, face danger, uncertainty, and moral ambiguity on a regular basis. Their work is vital, yet cloaked in secrecy. Despite the challenges they face, thousands of VAJA operatives continue to serve their country with courage, dedication, and unwavering resolve.

Tense Cooperation

The VAJA and the Islamic Revolutionary Guard Corps (IRGC), or Pasdaran in Farsi, form the two pillars of Iran's civilian and military intelligence establishment. Understanding how these two groups interact, especially how the VAJA cooperates with the IRGC's Intelligence Office (IRGC-IO), requires digging into Iranian politics, security issues, and strategic objectives.

OPPOSITE: The United States labeled the IRGC, one of the most powerful military-like forces in the Middle East, as a terrorist group in 2019.

The VAJA, Iran's main civilian intelligence agency, conducts domestic as well as foreign intelligence operations. Its job is to collect intelligence and counterintelligence and to defend the regime against internal and outside threats. The VAJA operates somewhat on its own but is overseen by the supreme leader, Ayatollah Ali Khamenei. It has a network of operatives and informants inside and outside Iran.

Meanwhile, the parallel military force, the IRGC, defends the purity of the Islamic Republic and the principles of the Islamic Revolution. Also created following the 1979 Islamic Revolution, the IRGC has become an important power. It has an extensive reach across different sections of Iranian society. The IRGC-IO is a key intelligence gathering and covert operation

Capturing Rigi

Abdolmalek Rigi led a Sunni resistance organization called Jundallah. Also known as the "Soldiers of God," the group operated in southeastern Iran. Jundallah was established in the early 2000s and fought to protect the Baluch Sunni minority community in Iran. Unfortunately, the organization used terrorist methods, such as bombings, abductions, and murders. The government of Iran and other Islamic countries declared Jundallah a terrorist organization and set out to find its leader. The hunt for Rigi was conducted by Iran's national security services, including the VAJA and the IRGC. In February 2010, through joint intelligence efforts, Rigi was located on a flight from Dubai to Kyrgyzstan. Iran forced the airplane to land, and intelligence forces arrested him. Rigi was executed in Iran in June 2010, which resulted in a significant setback for Jundallah.

unit supporting Iran's **proxy** forces and allies throughout the region.

The interaction between the VAJA and the IRGC-IO requires collaboration. Both agencies serve a common purpose, but they have separate orders and separate circles of influence. Sometimes the VAJA and the IRGC-IO pool their resources to solve a common problem. This collaboration is especially evident in national security, counterterrorism, and counterintelligence. For example, both agencies monitor dissident groups, counter foreign intelligence efforts, and fight extremists inside Iran. They also coordinate their activities supporting Iran's regional allies and proxy groups, such as Hezbollah in Lebanon, Hamas in the Palestinian territories, or other Shia **militias** in Syria and Iraq.

An example of the VAJA and the IRGC-IO collaborating is the joint effort in countering threats to Iran by ISIS (Islamic State of Iraq and Syria). In June 2017, ISIS attacked Iran's Parliament building and Ayatollah Khomeini's burial site in Tehran—both national symbols. Prior to the attacks, the extremist group had taken over a vast amount of territory in Iraq and Syria. As a country bordering both countries, Iran was in a strategically vulnerable position from the start.

The ISIS attacks forced the VAJA and the IRGC-IO to develop new methods of cooperation to combat a joint national security threat. They needed to pair the VAJA's specialized skills in gathering, decoding, and analyzing security data with the IRGC-IO's military intelligence capabilities. Working together, the two organizations identified potential ISIS members within Iran. Because the attacks were a rare breach of state security, the VAJA and the IRGC-IO took action in the form of nationwide raids against uncovered clusters of ISIS terrorists. The raids resulted in the detainment of dozens of suspects, the seizing of huge amounts of explosives, and the dismantling of numerous sleeper cells.

Despite this cooperation, the VAJA and the IRGC-IO compete for influence and resources inside the Iranian regime. This competition is caused by their overlap of responsibilities and different organizational cultures. As a civilian intelligence agency, the VAJA tends to place a high value on diplomacy, human intelligence (HUMINT) gathering, and maintaining some deniability. The IRGC-IO,

Top IRGC officer Qasem Soleimani was killed by a U.S. airstrike in 2020.

Ayatollah Ali Khamenei, Iran's supreme leader since 1989

in contrast, operates with a heavy reliance on paramilitary means such as **sabotage** and use of its proxy militias.

This competition sometimes creates friction. Such tensions sometimes result in turf battles, information-sharing disputes, or covert operations involving each other's undercover sources. Despite these occasional tensions, both agencies ultimately answer to the supreme leader. He reviews disputes between them and ensures the agencies are operating in alignment with the regime's broader goals.

Also, the relationship between the VAJA and the IRGC-IO is dynamic and can shift according to internal and external forces. Changes in leadership, geopolitical alliance changes, and new security threats can all affect the nature of their interaction. Both agencies also know how to change tactics and strategies to adapt to changing political landscapes and to remain relevant within the Iranian regime.

esc
delete
enter
return
shift
alt
option

Tactics and Tradecraft

Since its start in 1983, the VAJA has carved out a fierce reputation for itself through a series of daring missions and covert operations. It has acquired a vast international network of operatives and informants.

OPPOSITE: Computer spying, called cyberespionage, has become a VAJA strength in recent years.

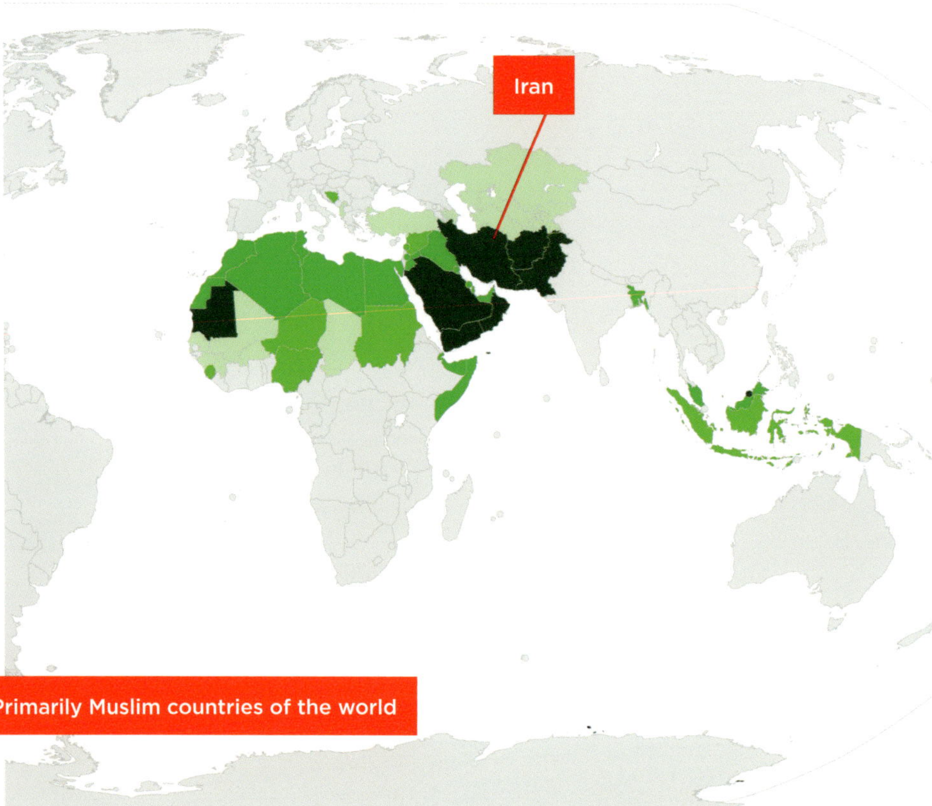

Primarily Muslim countries of the world

The VAJA uses a variety of tactics to conduct its intelligence abroad, from traditional methods to cyberwarfare and support of proxy groups. HUMINT is the world's oldest spy method. It relies on individuals using deception, trickery, and a few other tools. It entails recruiting and handling agents and informants in target countries and conducting covert operations to obtain sensitive information. The VAJA also trains and supports proxy militias and organizations supporting Iran's fight against Western influence in the region. These groups are force multipliers for VAJA intelligence operations. This means that they act as local extensions of Iran's intelligence network outside of Iran. The groups can be quickly mobilized for sabotage, terrorism, and irregular warfare.

Realizing the growing significance of the digital battlefield, today's VAJA gathers ELINT (electronic intelligence) via the Internet and computer monitoring, or hacking. It develops cyberwarfare and cyberespionage capabilities to hack into foreign governments, steal sensitive information, and conduct cyberattacks against Iran's enemies. The VAJA also collects SIGINT (signal intelligence) by intercepting radio, telephone, and other communications and PHOTINT (photographic intelligence) by studying photos taken by spy aircraft or human operatives. Because of the rapidly expanding role technology plays in the world of espionage, modern spies need a wide range of computer skills and support.

There are two main types of spy: legal and illegal. Legals work openly in their own country's embassy in a foreign country. Many VAJA operatives work out of Iranian embassies, consulates, and cultural centers around the

Operation Muddy Water

In 2017, the VAJA conducted a cyberespionage operation called "Muddy Water." It focused on government, telecommunications, and energy sectors across the Middle East, Europe, and North America. The infectious agent—Muddy Water—used spear-phishing as its primary method of attack. To chosen targets, it sent tailored emails containing harmful attachments or links. Disguised as corporate mail or important notifications, the emails triggered the installation of damaging software, called malware, on the target system when a user opened the attachment or clicked the link. The malware included various custom-built tools. These tools helped VAJA cyberintelligence operators create secret "backdoor" channels to the infected systems, hide their activity, change or destroy information from remote countries, monitor users' movements, and systematically remove the most valuable data without being discovered.

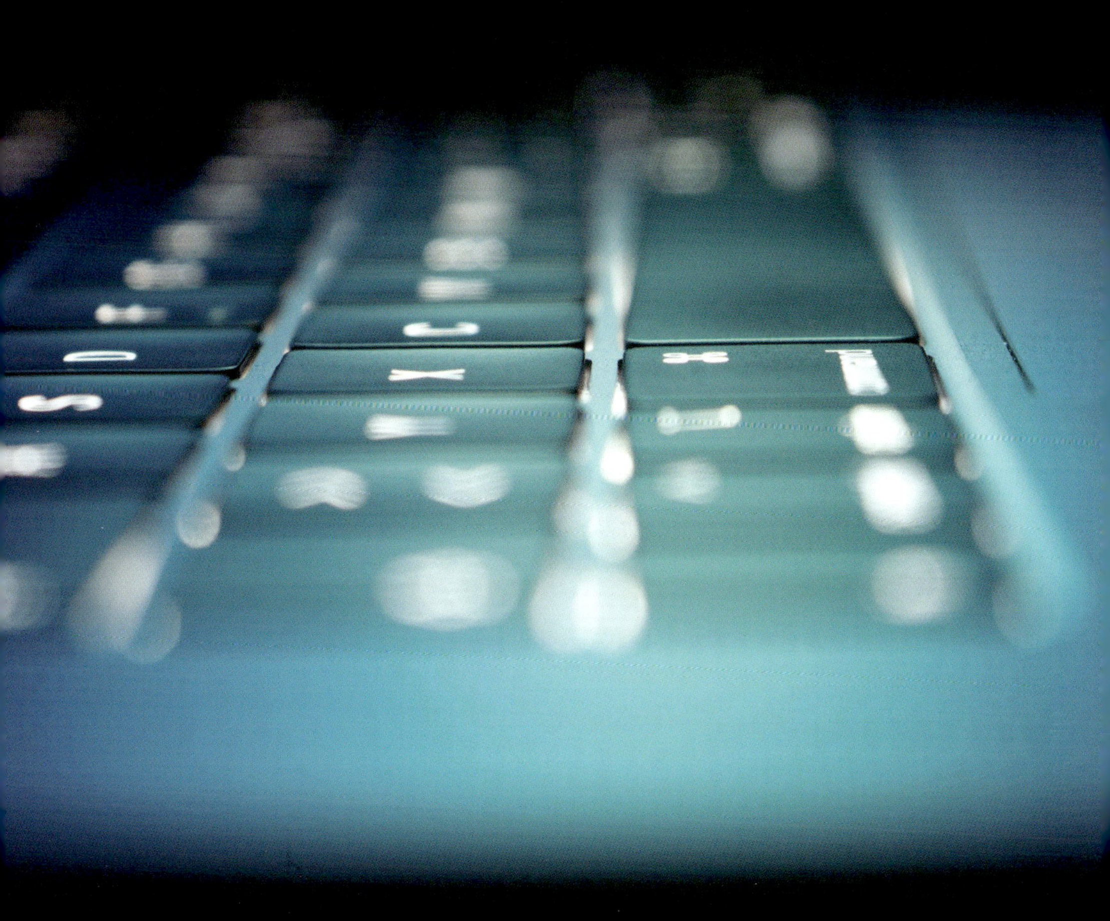

Iranian embassy in Budapest, Hungary

world. These are ideal sites for intelligence gathering. In their roles as official government employees, legals have access to sensitive information and powerful contacts in target countries. If they're caught spying or trying to recuit others, they are usually sent back to their home country rather than jailed.

Illegals, on the other hand, take on false identities and work undercover. **Moles** are a kind of illegal. VAJA moles work secretly inside an enemy's intelligence agency, such as the Mossad, or top-secret facility and relay confidential information back to Iran.

Iranian missiles light up the night sky over Israel in 2024.

Target: Israel

On April 13, 2024, Iran launched its largest **drone** and missile attack to date on Israel. More than 300 drones and ballistic missiles were fired overnight in response to a suspected Israeli drone strike on an Iranian diplomatic facility in Syria two weeks earlier. This was the first time Iran's military had fired directly at Israel, and it indicated a critical point in the long-standing "shadow war" between the two countries. Israel and its allies claimed they intercepted "99 percent" of the missiles, and no Israeli fatalities were reported. Afterward, both VAJA and IRGC-IO agents were likely tasked with obtaining information related to Israel's next move and the potential for escalating regional conflict, but such involvement would have been highly classified.

If an illegal is caught, punishment is often severe—from torture to execution.

As part of its job to protect the Islamic Republic, the VAJA conducts **propaganda** and influence campaigns through state-controlled media outlets, social networking sites, and cultural institutions. Controlled messaging is used to shape public opinion, influence political discourse, and control the Islamic Republic's narrative on important issues.

“THE VAJA CONDUCTS PROPAGANDA AND INFLUENCE CAMPAIGNS THROUGH STATE-CONTROLLED MEDIA OUTLETS, SOCIAL NETWORKING SITES, AND CULTURAL INSTITUTIONS.”

Over the years, the VAJA has used a wide range of tactics, including terrorism, to conduct operations around the world. Some of its missions have drawn international attention and condemnation. These include the 1992 bombing of the Israeli Embassy in Buenos Aires, Argentina, and the 1994 bombing of the AMIA (a Jewish community center), also in Buenos Aires. In the first explosion (a car bomb), 29 people were killed, and more than 250 were injured. The bombing two years later killed 87 people and injured more than 100. These acts were allegedly carried out by Hezbollah—Iran's Lebanon proxy and member of its "**Axis of Resistance**."

The VAJA is also suspected of the assassinations of Kurdish dissidents and opposition figures in Germany, Iraq, and Turkey. In addition to Hezbollah, the VAJA has provided financial assistance and support to militant groups in the Middle East, including Hamas in Palestine, the Houthi Movement in Yemen, and Shiite militias in Syria and Iraq.

A fighter for the militant group Hamas

Department 15

Within the VAJA lies a fearsome group of assassins known as Department 15. Specializing in "wetwork," a word sometimes used for assassination that refers to the spilling of blood, the top-secret group's primary mission is to hunt down and eliminate threats to the state. Its activities are rarely recorded or captured, and detailed information about its activities is scarce, given the extremely sensitive nature of its operations.

OPPOSITE: Members of VAJA's Department 15 operate largely in the shadows.

OPPOSITE Hasan-i Sabbah's group is said to have assassinated nearly 50 military, royal, and holy men during his lifetime.

The creation of Department 15 traces its origins to an 11th century group of Nizari Ismaili assassins who came from the mountains of Persia and Syria. Commanded by spiritual leaders known as imams, the assassins established a series of mountaintop forts in what is now modern-day southeastern Iran and Syria. From there they launched daring military campaigns against their enemies.

One of the most famous figures in Nizari history was Hasan-i Sabbah. He was a fascinating leader who founded a select group of fighters called fedayeen, or "those who sacrifice themselves." These fedayeen formed the Order of Assassins, also known as the Hashashiyyin. The Hashashiyyin became known for their brutal methods. They were tasked with killing political leaders, military leaders, and other high-profile figures they considered to be a threat. Hashashiyyin assassins

The 1979 Islamic Revolution led to armed street fighting throughout Iran.

snuck behind enemy lines and waited for the right time to strike. Under Sabbah, the Hashashiyyin carried out a campaign of terror against rival rulers, scaring away their foes and influencing intelligence agencies and military leaders across the generations.

Following the 1979 Islamic Revolution, as the young country found itself confronted by threats from all sides, the creators of the VAJA soon realized the need for additional protection. Within the new intelligence agency, a special unit was needed, one capable of conducting

Hasan-i Sabbah

the organization's most dangerous and deadly missions. Drawing inspiration from the storied legacy of the Order of Assassins, Department 15 adopted the role of the ancient Hashashiyyin. It prioritized deception, stealth, and ruthlessness to achieve its goals.

This modern version of Sabbah's fedayeen soon turned into one of the deadliest weapons in the Islamic

"DRAWING INSPIRATION FROM THE STORIED LEGACY OF THE ORDER OF ASSASSINS, DEPARTMENT 15 ADOPTED THE ROLE OF THE ANCIENT HASHASHIYYIN."

Republic's arsenal. It carried out a variety of deadly covert operations to neutralize threats to the regime and advance Iran's interests abroad. Today, Department 15 is the tip of the VAJA spear, and it operates as quietly and cunningly as the Hashashiyyin of ancient Persia. Its operatives are trained in the arts of deception, espionage, and killing, ready to use their skills in defense of the Islamic Republic and its revolutionary ideals.

The "chain murders" are perhaps the most well-known operations conducted by Department 15. The series of systematic assassinations targeted dissidents, intellectuals, and opposition activists in Iran from 1988 to 1998. They were characterized by their methodical nature and designed to instill fear and silence dissent. Those murdered by Department 15 assassins included writers, political activists, journalists, and ordinary citizens suspected of having anti-regime feelings. The methods used in carrying out the chain murders were brutal. Victims were often kidnapped and found dead with mutilated, tortured bodies at their homes or workplaces. Some were shot execution style. Others were strangled or poisoned. All of the deaths were meant to terrify anyone who dared question the regime's authority.

Department 15 operatives were given the freedom to target any perceived enemies of Iran following the

Chain murder victim Dariush Forouhar was an Iranian politician who spoke out against human rights abuses by the Islamic Republic.

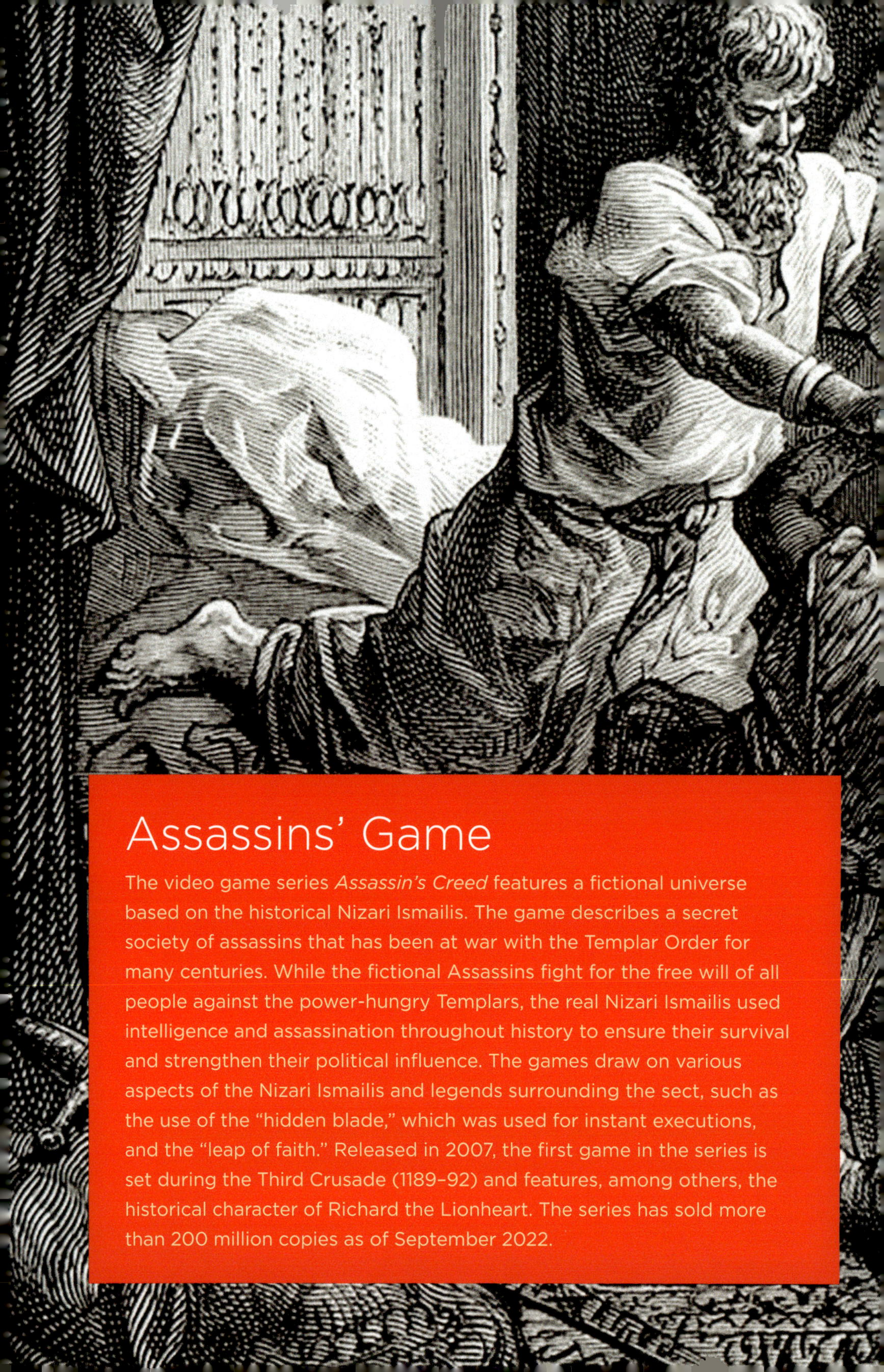

Assassins' Game

The video game series *Assassin's Creed* features a fictional universe based on the historical Nizari Ismailis. The game describes a secret society of assassins that has been at war with the Templar Order for many centuries. While the fictional Assassins fight for the free will of all people against the power-hungry Templars, the real Nizari Ismailis used intelligence and assassination throughout history to ensure their survival and strengthen their political influence. The games draw on various aspects of the Nizari Ismailis and legends surrounding the sect, such as the use of the "hidden blade," which was used for instant executions, and the "leap of faith." Released in 2007, the first game in the series is set during the Third Crusade (1189–92) and features, among others, the historical character of Richard the Lionheart. The series has sold more than 200 million copies as of September 2022.

Daggers were the weapons of choice for Department 15's predecessor, the Hashashiyyin.

SEEKING INFORMATION

MAJID DASTJANI FARAHANI

DESCRIPTION

Alias: Majid Farahani

Date(s) of Birth Used: July 26, 1982	**Place of Birth:** Iran
Hair: Brown and Gray	**Eyes:** Brown
Sex: Male	**Occupation:** Iranian Intelligence Officer
Nationality: Iranian	**Languages:** Farsi, English, Spanish, French

REMARKS

Farahani has ties to or may visit Iran and Venezuela.

DETAILS

Majid Dastjani Farahani, an Iranian intelligence officer, is wanted for questioning in connection with the recruitment of individuals for various operations in the United States, to include lethal targeting of current and former United States Government officials as revenge for the killing of IRGC-QF Commander Qasem Soleimani. Farahani also reportedly recruited individuals for surveillance activities focused on religious sites, businesses, and other facilities in the United States. Farahani acted or purported to act for or on behalf of, directly or indirectly, Iran's Ministry of Intelligence and Security.

If you have any information concerning this person, please contact your local FBI office or the nearest American Embassy or Consulate.

A U.S. intelligence agency request for information about an Iranian operative

Iran-Iraq War (1980–88), a period of increased political repression as well as social unrest in Iran. And they did exactly that. Over the course of almost a decade, countless innocent people were killed by VAJA assassins.

It wouldn't be until the late 1990s, as internal pressure and international scrutiny mounted, that the Islamic Republic would acknowledge the scale of its involvement in the chain murders. In 1999, then-President Mohamed Khatami called for an official inquiry. It resulted in the detention and prosecution of a number of VAJA agents. The trials were a step in the right direction, but they didn't give complete justice to the victims and their families, many of whom continue to look for answers.

Despite facing international condemnation and punishments, the VAJA remains an important part of Iran's security system and foreign policy agenda. Its operatives continue to assist Iran in projecting regional influence. They advance its strategic interests and combat perceived threats to the Islamic Republic wherever such threats may emerge.

The Muslim holy book, the Koran

Selected Bibliography

Beckhusen, Robert. "Iran Targets Dissidents with 30,000-Strong Spy Army [Updated]." WIRED. January 7, 2013. https://www.wired.com/2013/01/iranian-spies.

Bergman, Ronen. *The Secret War with Iran: The 30-Year Clandestine Struggle against the World's Most Dangerous Terrorist Power.* New York: Free Press, 2008.

Bob, Yonah Jeremy. "How the IRGC Overtook Iran's Intelligence Ministry." *The Jerusalem Post.* November 9, 2020. https://www.jpost.com/middle-east/how-the-irgc-overtook-irans-intelligence-ministry-648542.

Kahana, Ephraim, and Muhammad Suwaed. *Historical Dictionary of Middle Eastern Intelligence.* Lanham, Md.: Scarecrow Press, 2009.

Landale, James. "Israel-Gaza Briefings: Have Iran-Israel Missile Strikes Changed the Middle East?" BBC. April 27, 2024. https://www.bbc.com/news/world-middle-east-68900571.

Liu, Nicholas. "The Medieval Sect That Inspired the Video Game 'Assassin's Creed.'" *Smithsonian Magazine*. October 10, 2023. https://www.smithsonianmag.com/history/the-medieval-sect-that-inspired-the-video-game-assassins-creed-180983032.

Glossary

agent	a person who works for, but is not necessarily officially employed by, an intelligence service
Axis of Resistance	an Iranian-led Islamist group, including Syria, Hamas (Palestine), the Hezbollah movement (Lebanon), the Houthi movement (Yemen), and various Shi'ite armed group (Iraq), whose purpose is to stop Israeli and Western influence in the Middle East
counterintelligence	efforts made by a nation's intelligence agency to catch and eliminate spies working against the country and protect the country against sabotage or terrorism; also called counterespionage
dissident	someone who rebelliously disagrees, usually against a government
drone	an uncrewed aircraft, often directed by remote control, that is used to take secret photographs of or attack targets
espionage	the act of spying
Farsi	the modern-day language of Iran and western Afghanistan

intelligence	information uncovered and transmitted by a spy
militia	a private group of armed individuals that acts like an army, typically motivated by politics or religion
mole	an employee of one intelligence service who actually works for another service or who works undercover in a foreign country to supply intelligence
operative	an undercover agent working for an intelligence agency
pragmatic	practical or sensible
propaganda	material distributed to promote a government's or group's point of view or to damage an opposing point of view; some propaganda is untrue or unfairly exaggerated
proxy	given the authority to represent another and act on its behalf
recruit	to hire or enlist
regime	a form of government
sabotage	the act of purposely damaging or destroying something, especially for political or military gain
sleeper cell	a group of operatives placed in a target country or organization long before they're asked to actively spy
tradecraft	the procedures, techniques, and devices used by spies to carry out their activities

Websites

Explainer: Tactics of Iranian Intelligence

https://iranprimer.usip.org/blog/2023/feb/17/explainer-how-iran%E2%80%99s-intelligence-agencies-work
Dive deep into the operation of Iran's intelligence agencies.

The International Spy Museum

https://www.spymuseum.org
Explore bios of real-life agents and frequently asked questions about spying.

Iran

https://www.britannica.com/place/Iran
Learn about the country's land, economy, and people.

Index